Basketball Tips A

You want to make it on the middle school basketball team? You want to make it on the High School basketball team? You want to make it on the college basketball ball team or do you want to make to the NBA? Well if you do then your first step starts here by reading and following everything in this book. If you're a serious baller then this book is as important as eating to you. Because when you eat, you live for another day and when you make it to the NBA you make enough money to live every day. Out of all the other training books this one is the most complete guide to every aspect of basketball. This book will guarantee improve your game and give you a shot at making it to the league. But if you do want to make it to the NBA then it starts now, right here because every knowledge that you need are all here. This book explains ball handling tips, passing, defense, rebounding, shooting and more. So get up out of the bed or off the couch and get to work. The time is now because if wait too long then the time is late.

Ball Handling Drills

The secret to getting ball handling skills is to gain strength and power in your fingertips, wrist and forearms for confident control of the ball and by dribbling the ball for a couple hours. But you have to give your fingers, wrist and forearms a little rest between exercises. Work on them no more than 5 days a week. Otherwise you'll be overworking and tiring your muscles. Like lifting weights, you need rest every other day but you still can play ball every day. So you're best option is to make a schedule of your workouts; for example, this is how I build my handles; on Mondays I work on strengthening my fingers by doing finger exercises. On Tuesdays I work on my wrists by doing wrist exercises. And Wednesdays is my forearms. Thursdays I start over again with my fingers but you can fix your schedule how you want it.

Things That Improve Your Dribbling

Stretching: Stretching fingers is as important as any other body parts. You can stretch your fingers before you play by balling your hand into a fist and then open it as wide as possible. Do this ten times.

Tennis ball: By bouncing the tennis ball you work on eye and hand coordination and by squeezing it you can strengthen your fingers.

Push-ups: Push-ups helps by strengthening your forearms

Typing: By typing for 10 minutes straight, you build muscles in your fingers. It is a good idea to type for 10-20 minutes of day.

Videos: Yes playing video games may help because it stretches your fingers and strengthens your thumb but that don't mean you should spend a lot of time on playing video games. But a good half of hour is a day is okay.

Sweeping: Don't be lazy when your mom tells you to sweep the floor, look at it as you're getting ball handling exercise by sweeping. It improves forearm strength so try to do at least 100 sweeps a day and also if you want to improve control when spinning the ball on your fingers try balancing the broom on your fingers for up to 1 minute then increase the time until you can master it.

Writing: If you train yourself to write with both hands it can help you dribble with your weak hand as well. For example, if you are right handed, try writing with your left hand for 10 minutes a day for a month and you'll notice you had improve dribbling with your left/weak hand. And I know this because I'm considered to have one of the best handles in the world.

Dishes: I know you probably think this is a joke but by washing dishes, after finger exercises, you really relax your fingers from the warm hot water in the sink. So when your mom tells you to do your chores, you should be more welcome to do it. It's like you give yourself a foot bath so is washing dishes is like giving yourself a hand bath.

Crossover technique

A crossover is a good move to add to your game. It creates space giving you more room for a jump shot or a pass.

Crossover: Change directions by pushing off with the "outside" foot and dribbling the ball low and hard with the corresponding hand over to the opposite dribbling hand.

Spin Move: Change directions by reverse-pivoting off of the "inside" foot to perform a reverse pivot. The quickest way to do this is to start the pivot when the "inside" foot is forward. That way, the "outside" leg is already part of the way to the new direction. If you start the pivot when the inside foot is back, then your outside leg has to cover far more distance in the spin and it will be easier for a defender to get a back tip. As you reverse pivot, pull the ball with your dribbling hand over into position to be dribbled by your other hand. The more you can get the ball pulled over toward that hand and protected by your body, the less chance there will be for a back tip.

The spin move has the disadvantage of being more vulnerable to blind double teams than other change-of-direction techniques, but it can be an effective weapon when used with adequate court vision.

Behind-the-Back: Change directions by dribbling the ball the ball behind your back. Footwork is critical here. The behind-the-back dribble begins as the outside leg is back and just beginning to move forward, and the ball needs to be dribbled all the way over to the opposite hand. The key to an effective behind-the-back dribble is to continue moving forward rather than just dribbling sideways. For this to happen, the arms and legs need to be coordinated so that the ball can get where it needs to go. This is an advanced skill, but most effective point guards have it.

Between-the-Legs: Change directions by dribbling the ball between your legs to your other hand. There are two ways to do this:

•You dribble the ball backwards between your legs while your inside leg is forward. This move will create some space for you to change directions, but it will slow you down a step or two, too. This is by far the most common form of dribbling between your legs.

•You dribble the ball forward between your legs while your outside leg is forward. You will push off that same leg in the new direction.

The ball is momentarily exposed in this technique, so it is best used when you have a good cushion from the defender. With this technique, you don't lose forward momentum. Though it has limited applications, this move does allow for an element of surprise.

Between-the-Legs Followed by Behind-the-Back: This is a combo technique that ends up with you going in the same direction after a momentary decoy move. First, you perform the 'inside leg forward' version of the between-the-legs dribble; as soon as the ball reaches your other hand, you immediately use that hand to dribble behind your back over to your initial dribbling hand. It's a good change-of-pace technique.

Once your players master these techniques, they will have great tools for putting the ball on the floor against pressure. The two main goals should be to perform the skills well in both directions and to perform them without looking at the ball.

Power dribbling drills

Basketball players first learn to dribble the basketball with one hand, then to alternate hands, and progressively to increase to more advanced dribbling. As a basketball player, a powerful and effective way to keep defenders on their toes and increase your threat as an offensive player is to develop an agile and quick dribbling technique. The power dribble can do this.

A basic power dribble is when you dribble the ball at a very intense rate. Maintain your normal form and posture. Use your muscles to thrust the ball forcefully down, and then expect the ball to quickly bounce back to your hand.

The drills described below will help you gain confidence and agility to handle a basketball in a power dribble. This will help you run a fast break, cut through the defensive, and outmaneuver your opponents.

1. **Power crossover**- Power dribble in your right hand, and then quickly bounce the ball to your left hand. Power dribble with your left hand for a few seconds before bouncing the ball back to your right hand.

2. **Dribble Blindfolded** - Wrap a cloth around your head as a blindfold, or you could simply close your eyes...no peeking. Power dribble a ball for at least 60 seconds. This drill helps you enhance your tactile sense of the ball. You can enhance the drill by performing it in the center of a deserted basketball court, walking around while dribbling. To make the drill even more challenging, try power dribbling two balls, one in each hand, while being blindfolded and slowly walking around a deserted basketball court.

3. **10-5 Repeats** - This drill exercises power dribbling with one hand at a time. Choose which hand your would like to practice. Power dribble for 10 seconds, then soft dribble for 5

seconds. Repeat multiple times. This exercise teaches your arm muscles how to alternate between various dribbling speeds that occur during game play.

4. **Dribble Between Legs While Walking** - In order to do this drill you will need a segment of floor, such as a basketball court floor, a street's sidewalk, or a wide hallway that is deserted. Power dribble while walking up and down the walkway, power dribble the ball between your legs to practice fancy dribbling skills. To enhance the drill, perform the drill at a quicker walking pace, maybe at a light jogging pace

When to end your dribbling

Once you end your dribble, you cannot dribble again. You are literally nailed to the spot where you have ended it. This situation can provide the opponent guarding you with an advantage. Knowing you cannot dribble, the defender can be all over you, making it very difficult for you to pass or shoot. If you are outside your shooting range, your opponent can drop off to help teammates.

To avoid this situation, end your dribble only at the moment you choose to execute a pass or a shot. When advancing the ball with a dribble, you can stop moving, but keep dribbling. For example, you start to drive towards the hoop. Suddenly, there is congestion ahead. Stop, but keep your dribble

Defense tips and drills

Defense is 90 percent heart and 10 percent skill, and your success is determined by your will and commitment to the task. That being said, there are a few teaching points to remember when playing perimeter defense on the ball:

Stay Low

Remember to begin with your shoulders lower than the person you are guarding. We call this the shoulders game. By keeping your shoulders lower at the start and then continuously throughout the penetration and drive, you are more likely to get to the spot before the offense.

An Arm's Length

Do not begin too close or too far away from the offense. If you are too close, they will drive by you. If you are too far, they will shoot. The best thing is to begin at least an arm's length away. It is appropriate to reach out to your defender if you are not sure whether you are far enough away.

Keep Steps Short

Never forget your footwork. Taking long steps often will hinder your progress while defending drives. Take shorter, choppier steps and remember to "push-pull" off your front foot.

Remember the Hands

Another key is to have active hands. While on the ball your hands are busy, but you must also remember to use your hands while defending the penetration. Use a "deflection hand" high and a "ball hand" low and up on your defender. A lot of coaches will call this "riding" a player out. While you are defending the drive, try to poke the ball out with your ball hand, and then use your deflection hand to block passes or quick shots.

Swipe Up

Another important hint is to never hit down on the ball. When you swing down on the ball it is a more aggressive motion and more likely to get attention from the officials for a called foul. Swipe up on the ball.

Get in Shape

The most successful defenders will have strong core muscles. Your hips, abs and buttocks will be strong and help you be balanced and able to move quickly in lateral motions. Jumping rope will help your foot speed.

The best way to become a great defender, of course, is to know your opponent. Watch film and read scouting reports. The best defender is the smartest defender.

Improve your rebounding

Run to the Front of the Basket on Your Fast Break

If you want to encounter a lot of offensive rebounds, run to the front of the basket during your fast break. This is a great time to do so because the defense is not in position for the rebound yet.

Run to the Front of the Rim on the Dribble Drive

During dribble penetration, follow your teammate to the rim so you can be there to retrieve the ball if he misses. This is a great time to rebound because the defense usually collapses on the drive and they forget to block out. This will allow you to get more offensive rebounds as well as points.

Practice Drills That Teach You to Rebound Outside Your Area

Great rebounders go for the ball no matter where it's at. Bad rebounders stand and watch because they think the ball it out of their reach.

You can teach yourself to rebound out of your area by running basketball rebounding drills that make you go a long ways to get the ball. For example, throw the ball off the back board on the other side of the rim and "go get it!"

Make Contact Before Your Opponent

You will be able to be in control of what happens if you make contact first when boxing out. Make sure to hit them first before they make contact with you to ensure leverage. Remember, anticipate and always be first. This will give you the edge.

Start Moving as the Shooter is Uncoiling

If you react and mover quicker, you will improve anticipation and get more rebounds. As the shooter is uncoiling start the contact by blocking out. Do the same on offense; as the shooter uncoils go after the rebound. You will get more rebounds!

Passing tips

Types of Passes

There are essentially two types of passes:

Air Pass - The pass travels between players without hitting the floor.

Bounce Passes - The pass is thrown to the floor so that it   bounces to the intended receiver.

Each type of pass comes with its own variations.

Basic Variations:

Chest Pass

Bounce Pass

Overhead Pass

Wrap Around Pass

Advanced Variations:

Baseball Pass

Dribble Pass

Behind-the-Back Pass

Pick-and-Roll Pass

Basic Passes

CHEST PASS

The chest pass is named so because the pass originates from the chest. It is thrown by gripping the ball on the sides with the thumbs directly behind the ball. When the pass is thrown, the fingers are rotated behind the ball and the thumbs are turned down. The resulting follow through has the back of the hands facing one another with the thumbs straight down. The ball should have a nice backspin.

When throwing a chest pass, the players should strive to throw it to the receiver's chest level. Passes that go low to high or high to low are difficult to catch.

BOUNCE PASS

The bounce pass is thrown with the same motion however it is aimed at the floor. It should be thrown far enough out that the ball bounces waist high to the receiver. Some say try to throw it 3/4 of the way to the receiver, and that may be a good reference point to start, but each player has to experiment how far to throw it so it bounces to the receiver properly. Putting a proper and consistent backspin on the pass will make the distance easier to judge.

OVERHEAD PASS

The overhead pass is often used as an outlet pass. Bring the ball directly above your forehead with both hands on the side of the ball and follow through. Aim for the teammate's chin. Some coaches advise not bring the ball behind your head, because it can get stolen and it takes a split-second longer to throw the pass.

WRAP AROUND PASS

Step around the defense with your non-pivot foot. Pass the ball with one hand (outside hand). It can be used as an air or a bounce pass. You will often see the wrap-around, air pass on the perimeter and the wrap-around, bounce pass to make an entry into the post

Advanced Passes

BASEBALL PASS

A baseball pass is a one-handed pass that uses the same motion as a baseball throw. This is often used to make long passes. Be careful with young kids. You don't want them throw their arms out.

DRIBBLE PASS

The dribble pass is used to quickly pass the ball with one hand off of the dribble. This can be an air or bounce pass. You'll see Steve Nash do this all of the time.

BEHIND-THE-BACK PASS

A behind-the-back pass is when you wrap the ball around your back to throw the ball. It is used to avoid the defender when making a pass across the front of you would be risky. It can also be used to throw the ball to a player trailing on the fast break.

I would not recommend kids to use this pass during a game until heavily practiced.

PICK AND ROLL PASS

This is a pass that is used when the defenders double-team or switch on the pick and roll. If dribbling to the right, your left side is facing the target and you bring the ball up from your right side to throw the ball overhead to the screener who has either rolled to the basket or popped to the perimeter. The pass is used to shield the ball from the defender, and many times is thrown in "hook shot" fashion. Advanced players can do this while slightly fading away from the defender.

Teaching Points

When teaching passing, points of emphasis should be:

☐ A good pass is a pass a teammate can catch.

- When passing, step toward your receiver.

- When catching, step toward the pass.

- Like shooting, the ball should have a backspin to it. This is accomplished by following through on every pass.

Passing Drills

Drill No. 1 -- Chest Pass

A simple and effective drill when coaching young players is to set them up in a circle of around five meters in diameter and have one player start off in the middle of the circle.

One of the players making up the circle starts with the ball and begins the drill by passing it to the player in the middle. They then follow their pass and move to the middle and as they do this, the middle player with the ball passes it to the next player in the circle and follows the ball again to take up their new position.

The passes must be chest passes delivered crisply to each other and they should look to catch the ball and pass it on without dropping it. Your players must continue to quickly pass and move in this manner for the entire drill and you can set different targets depending on the ability of your players. For example, you may ask for 50 passes to be completed before the ball touches the ground and if it is dropped before they have to start over.

This passing drill will get players used to quickly moving the ball on to each other and then moving which they will need to do in fast attacks.

Drill No. 2 –- Chest Pass

Another skill they need to be able to grasp is passing the ball while moving as they will not always be able to stop and pick out a pass during games.

One way to get your players passing and moving is to get them into pairs and have one partner from each form a line on the sideline with the other partners lining up opposite them with around a fifteen foot separation.

Each pair should start with one ball and they should side step down the court and every couple of steps pass the ball across to their partner. Young players may struggle to play an accurate pass to their partner with them both moving at first but through practice they will start passing to a moving target while they are moving which will become vitally important during games.

These two drills both utilize the chest pass and it is also an important part of basketball coaching to get your players used to distributing the ball using the bounce pass and the overhead pass as well so they can find a pass in all situations during games.

Drill No. 3 — Bounce Pass

The technique for the bounce pass is basically the same as the chest pass. The player holds the ball in front of their chest with their thumbs pointing up and their fingers forward. Like the chest pass they will step into the throw and push through the ball, however the bounce pass is a slower pass than the chest pass and they are of course looking to bounce the ball off the ground into their teammate's hands.

An easy way to practice the bounce pass is to get your players into pairs and stand them a few feet apart and tell them to aim for a spot about a quarter of the distance away from their partner. Through practice they will start to get a feel for where to bounce the ball and at what speed so that it is easy to receive and working in pairs will help them become comfortable with the skill before moving onto more complex drills.

Drill No. 4 — Overhead Pass

Practicing the overhead pass can be done in this way as well by pairing players up and going over the technique with them until they are comfortable with it. This time the ball starts above the player's head and they should keep their fingers up and thumbs back. As with the chest pass they should step into the throw and push through the ball aiming for their teammate's chest.

The overhead pass is used in games from stationary positions primarily such as in an inbound pass, passing after a rebound or an outlet pass. It is not used on the run so players need not practice moving and passing with the overhead pass.

Improving your player's passing skills is vital to the success of your team and it is especially important to develop passing ability within young players as they need to be able to do the basics on the court if they want to become better players. Getting your players used to quick and accurate passing and moving will make your offense much more potent and cause problems for defenses each game

Perfecting The Chest Pass

Stand about fifteen feet from a wall. Step forward with your right foot, snapping your wrists as you throw a chest pass at the wall. Repeat this, only step with your left foot the next time. It is important to be able to step with either foot when throwing a pass. If done correctly, the pass should hit the wall at a height roughly equivalent to the height of your chest. Do this fifty times.

Then proceed to throw fifty bounce passes. If thrown correctly, the ball should hit the floor 2/3's of the way between you and the person that you are throwing it to—or, in this case, the wall. The same fundamentals apply when throwing a bounce pass as with throwing a chest pass: snap your wrists, step into your pass, and keep your eyes focuses on where you are throwing the ball

One Hand Pass

First things first, I do not suggest that all players perform one-hand passes in games. It is much riskier to make a one-hand pass. Where-as a two-handed pass can be pulled back if need, a one-handed pass is final. The decision is made. Second, it is much harder to throw an accurate pass with only one hand.

That being said, I recommend practicing one-handed passes to each and every player. Why? Because the first rule of practice is this: make practice hard so the game is easy. Players should practice passing with one hand, just as players should practice dribbling two balls. If a player can dribble two basketballs with high energy and with great execution, then dribbling one basketball will be a piece of cake. Not only will their skills be better, but they will have more confidence as a result of their demanding training. The same is true of passing.

If a player can pass off the dribble with one hand with accuracy in practice, then they will definitely have the ability to pass accurately with two in games. On top of that, their confidence as a passer will be through the roof.

Ambidexterity

Very few players are born with the natural ability to use both hands equally, but every player can become ambidextrous to some extent. Therefore, the more a player forces him or herself to train both hands equally, the better each hand will get.

Practicing one-handed passes will not only make you a better passer, it will make your weak-hand dribbling stronger, and you will become an even better finisher around the basket, among other things, because you will be better with both hands. You will be amazed by the improvement of the rest of your game just by forcing both hands to individually pass the basketball.

Game Execution

Finally, you should practice passing with one hand, so you will actually have the ability to do so in a game. Just as it sometimes necessary to make a behind the back pass, or an imaginative finish at the basket, it is sometimes absolutely necessary to make a one-handed pass in a game. At times, it is the only way to get the ball to a shooter on time and on target.

The game of basketball is made up of inches and seconds. Sometimes the window of opportunity will be closed if a player has to take the time to pass with both hands. Pure and simple, it is a split second faster if a player can pass with one. Players who can't do so, will have limitations in crunch time.

No Limits

As players, we should never put limits on our game. We want to remain fundamental, but we also want our bodies to have the ability to do exactly what is required to make the best play each and every time. That's why practicing one-handed passes is so crucial; confidence will be gained, both hands will become more equal, and at the very least, we will never be limited by what we mistakenly labeled "not fundamental."

There is no need for great passes when ordinary passes will do. Pass to an open teammate, in an area he can catch it, away from the defense. If you cannot do that, don't throw the pass.

While we would all like every pass to be perfect, we all know that will not be the case. The receiver must go where he needs to go to catch the ball. This may seem unrelated, but, to draw a parallel, baseball players know that a great defensive 1st baseman makes great infielders. He covers up for bad throws and can make a shortstop a star. By emphasizing the catch, passers will become more confident and receivers more aggressive.

Shooting

Spot Shooting

One shooter with two balls and two rebounders. (Designate spots ahead of time e.g. 3pt line point, wing, baseline, elbow, etc.) Shooter stays in one spot and shoots for 30 seconds at each spot getting in as many shots as possible during the 30 seconds. Rotate spots so that everyone shoots from each designated spot.

Catch the ball on the wing, square up for 3 pt shot or put the ball on the floor with 2-3 dribbles either to corner of free throw line or to the baseline. Divide group in half with line of shooters under the basket and passers at the top of the key (point position). Shooting line can alternate sides with person breaking out from the low post block towards the 3 point line free throw line extended (wing position on offensive sets). Alternate lines.

21

Have players compete against each other or have teams (players) shoot from designated spot (3 pt line wing, elbow, etc); first shot (also known as the long shot) counts two points if made; get rebound off of made or missed shot and shoot a short shot which counts one point if made.

First player or team to 21 is the winner. Each player will shoot a total of two shots each timeone long shot and one short shot then pass the ball to next player or go back to the spot if playing game individually.

Hot Shot

Pick designated spots on the floor such as 3-point shots, elbow shots, low block shot, and lay-ups. Indicate a point value for each shot. (E.g. 3 pt shots worth five points, elbow shots worth three points, low block shots worth two points, and layups worth one point). The longer the shots, the more points they should be worth.

Each player shoots from any of the designated spots for a certain amount of time (30 seconds or one minute). Points are given (pre-determined values) for each made shot. High score wins. Some people can add the bonus points rule. Such as a player gets five bonus points if a shot is attempted from every spot within the time limit regardless of make or miss. This is to add incentive to shoot from every spot instead of just one or two spots.

Better 3pt Shooting

Warm-Up Speed

Jog (but never walk) through each of these shots. This will help you work up a sweat.

Start around five feet from the basket, and shoot untill you make a shot all-net before moving back one step. Repeat the process until you get all the way back to the 3-point line. Continue shooting until you make an all-net 3-pointer.

Initially, do this from the baseline and work your way back to the 3-point line in the corner.

Then do the other (right or left baseline) and finally go down the middle and finish with a 3-pointer from the top of the key. Finally, do your normal stretching routine.

Practice Speed

This next part of your practice shooting is best done with a rebounder and a passer. However, if shooting on your own, simply pass to yourself, shoot, rebound and speed dribble back to the spot.

You are now repeating the process of working your way back, only this time going as fast as you think you can, then speeding up your perception of what you think is going fast, and go even faster! Obviously this is great conditioning.

There are several kinds of footwork currently being used by good shooters. These include: the classic inside foot 1-2 step, the 2-foot jump stop, the plant rear foot and step-in, and hop into the shot (1-2 step or 2-foot jump stop).

Make one all-net shot of each of the following types of shots and work your way back from three distances: start at 10 feet out, then move to 15 feet and finally to 3-point range. Do both a catch-and-shoot and a shot off the dribble, moving left-right-center. That's six made all-net baskets from each spot.

As before, you must make an all-net shot before progressing to the next type of shot and distance.

Competitive Speed

This is the most important part of becoming a proficient shooter in actual games. Do this work-out with defenders. Learning this way will give you transference from practice to actual games. You'll play this way and it will be easy to make shots in games and at crunch time.

Have defenders close out on you (sometimes from closer than they will be in the game) to try and steal the ball and block the shot. Want to become a fearless shooter? Have the defender foul you on purpose. But this should be just a slap on the wrist or controlled nudge, so you don't get hurt. Make (again not just take) three shots like this during every practice and you will become a more focused "in the zone" shooter. You probably will also get to the free throw line in games and have a chance to make a 4-point play

To Prepare For A Perfect Shot

☐ **Low, Balanced Stance** -- players should "sit down," have their knees bent, with a lead foot forward to prepare for the catch. Players should be "under the ball" as they prepare to receive the pass.

☐ **Hands In Ready Position** -- hands should be in the position they will be on the shot, with the shooting hand under and behind the ball and the guide hand on the side. "Catch it the way you are going to shoot it."

☐ **Hand and Elbow Below The Ball** --
players should catch the ball with
their shooting hand and elbow
below the ball. This helps keep the
player low on the catch and helps to
prevent "dipping" the ball. The ball
swinging "down-up" creates
unnecessary action and causes the
shooting motion to work against
itself. With the shooting hand and
elbow tucked under the ball on the
catch, the player has already done
everything necessary to then begin
the shooting sequence.

☐ **Low to High** -- players should catch
in a low position and go from that
position into their shooting

51

sequence. When catching the ball in an upright position, players have a "High to Low" motion with their body. This adds time to the shooting sequence--meaning it now takes longer for a player to get off their shot. Against better defenders, this causes an open shot to become a contested shot and a contested shot to become a block. This "High to Low" body motion also leads to inconsistency in distance and trajectory, as well as to shot fatigue in late stages of games. Catching the ball in a good stance with the shooting hand and elbow under that ball takes the player from "Low to High" for a nice consistent shooting rhythm.

☐ **Straight Up, Straight Down --**
players should not fall forward or
backward on their shot. This leads
to inconsistency and missed shots
that should have been makes.
Balanced vertical elevation will lead
to more made shots. This can be
achieved by keeping the shoulders
directly in-line with the knees as
players leave the floor.

Freethrows

Free-throw shooting is like memorization: if
you do it enough, you can perform like a
machine. The key is to shoot free throws for
twenty minutes straight during this drill. Count
your makes and misses (i.e. 1-for-1, 1-for-2,
2-for-3, etc), in order to chart your
improvement over a period of time.

Shooting Free-Throws Properly

Although a large part of free-throw shooting is based on personal tendencies, a few procedures should be universally followed in order to achieve maximum success.

1.Line the foot that corresponds with your shooting hand--if you're right handed, your left foot--up with the nail that is nailed into the center of every free throw line in every gym. (If you are shooting outside, try to guess where the center of the foul line is.) This guarantees you a level of alignment with the rim, helpful to your overall success. Though there are exceptions to the rule, most great free-throw shooters follow this line of thinking (even if they won't admit it).

2.Fix your eyes on the front of the rim. Do not use the back of the rim, or, even worse, the white square on the backboard as your point of reference. Doing so means that you are looking towards a place on the basket where, if you hit them, you will most probably miss. Whereas, if you aim towards the front of the rim, your mind automatically tells you to shoot the ball at this point with a trajectory conducive to a friendly bounce. And even if you hit the front of the rim, if you have the rotation that you should as a shooter, the ball will roll into the basket.

Keys to Effectiveness

Repetition is the key to effectiveness. If you practice them enough, you will become a good free-throw shooter.

Jump-rope Exercises

One staple in the game of basketball and conditioning has long been the jump rope. While every tool has its place, the jump rope is a tool that I use regularly for two reasons:

• The natural rhythmic pattern of having to turn the rope and jump/bounce at the same time, there is a major coordination factor involved.

• Quick contacts with the feet force athletes to stay on the front half of their foot - thus improving the "elasticity" of the lower leg (this means quicker and more explosive!).

Here are 5 of my favorite and most effective jump rope drills:

Quick Feet

While this isn't the most exciting variation of jump roping, it's perhaps the most important. You will simply start with both feet on the ground at the same time while you're turning the rope as quickly as you possibly can. Do not underestimate the effectiveness of this drill. This is a great starting point if you aren't able to currently jump rope and if you are a master you can always work at improving your quickness.

Lateral Quick Feet

This variation is the exact same as the above drill except you're going to move side to side instead of just up and down. This will help improve your ability to move laterally. This is a great starting point for improving the foot/ankle complex to control stability (balance and control) while being quick.

Ali Shuffle

With this drill you will start with your feet staggered (one foot forward and one foot backward). You will then jump up and switch the feet so that you now have your other foot forward. Continue in this pattern working at contacting the ground at the same time with both feet.

The Ali shuffle will help greatly with learning to recover with one foot forward (much like defense).

Hurdle Step

Start with one leg off the ground with the knee up toward waist height. You will hold that leg up and in position while hopping up and down on the other foot.

This drill is great for improving single-leg power and elasticity. Make sure you start with shorter times (or fewer reps) with this drill as the stress on the lower leg is MUCH higher than the double leg versions listed above. Too much single-leg jump roping can cause shin splints!

Lateral Hurdle Step

This is exactly the same as above except you are jumping side to side while on the one leg. This is very challenging as it incorporates stability in the foot/ankle complex.

Bonus Exercise - Double Jumps

If you're already good at jump roping and you're looking to improve your jumping ability one of the best drills I know are the double jumps. Start like Quick Feet except instead of doing only one turn of the rope you will make two turns of the rope each time you jump.

Because of the height you are jumping it works great at improving the power in the lower leg (picture higher jumps).

As a general rule I like jump roping drills to last about 10-30 seconds if you're trying to improve your quickness or jumping ability. As you get better, do more sets/reps of the 10-30s intervals and shrink your rest time in between sets. Below you will find a sample 10-minute program:

- Quick Feet: 3 x 30s, rest 15s between each 30s rep

- Lateral Quick Feet 3 x 30s, rest 15s between each 20s rep

- Ali Shuffle 3 x 30s, rest 15s between each 30s rep

- Hurdle Step 3 x 5s, each leg, rest 10s

- Lateral Hurdle Step 3 x 5s, each leg, rest 10s

- Double Jumps 2 x 10 (20 total)

Explosive Step

The following three drills will improve your quickness, agility and reaction time. Perform two to three of these drills twice a week during the offseason. The time each drill is performed and the rest time between sets can transform each drill from a quickness drill to a conditioning drill. Because there's a time and place for conditioning, make sure to stick to the prescribed times to keep these drills improving your quickness so you can achieve the most benefit for your first-step and scoring ability.

Ball Drop

Benefits: Footwork, hand quickness, eye-hand coordination

Reps: 30 seconds

Sets: 4-6

Make sure you're in a defensive stance.

Rest: 60-90 seconds

Instructions:

- Stand arms length away from partner in defensive stance
- Partner holds tennis ball in each hand
- Sprint to ball after partner's throw
- Catch ball before second bounce

- Toss back to partner and sprint back to starting position

- React and sprint to next throw from partner

- Partner should vary distance, direction and speed of throws

Coaching Point: Your partner should vary the hand he uses on throws and constantly change-up the pattern. For example, throw left hand, left hand, left hand and then right hand because it's much more unpredictable then throwing left hand, right hand, left hand. This forces you to react faster and improve your first-step.

Block to Block

Benefits: Lateral quickness and agility

Reps: 12-15 seconds

Sets: 4-6

Rest: 60-90 seconds

Instructions:

☐ Stand in lane in athletic position between the blocks

☐ Partners kneels at top of key behind three point line with two tennis balls

☐ Partner rolls one ball to either block

☐ Defensive slide to block, tap ball back to partner, slide back to starting position

☐ React to next roll and repeat

Coaching Point: Don't ever cross your feet and make sure to stay low with your chest up and your hands up and active. You have to stay low to the ground so you can reach the ball and tap it back to your partner. Your hands should be in front and active like they are in a game so you can catch a pass or grab a rebound. If your hands are in by your sides you can't do these things in a game and you can't perform this drill. And most importantly, work hard. Your intensity of effort during this drill is crucial.

Star Drill

Benefits: Reaction and short burst quickness

Reps: 15 seconds

Sets: 4-6

Rest: 60-90 seconds

Instructions:

- Place five cones around three point line

- Perform athletic movement such as backboard taps, or defensive slides from block to block

- When partner calls number of cone, sprint to cone, challenge an imaginary shot, and back pedal back to starting spot

- Continue performing original movement

- React to partner's next call and sprint to and from cone

- Repeat

Coaching Point: Adjust the drill by sprinting to the cone as if you are closing out on a shooter. Chop your feet as you get close to the cone, get low and keep a hand up to put a hand in the imaginary shooters face. Then sprint back to the start. You can also change the movement pattern used such as sprinting to the cone and then backpedaling back to the start. Each different movement helps work another part of your game.

OTHER BOOKS TO READ

Project Dreams

In this story, two twins (Rasheed and Shareef) have dreams of making it out of the hopeless ghetto but many obstacles get in their way that make their dreams further away.

The Punisher

This is a story about a middle age man who punishes people for bad morals they have or for doing ungodly things, then he realizes later that he was no different from them and set out to punish people differently.

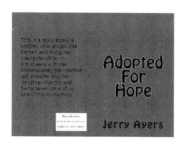

Adopted for Hope

This is a story about a mother who prostitutes herself and her young daughter and then when she gets arrested, one of her new customers takes her daughter in.

This book here discuss the
real meaning of Nigger, Black,
African, African American
and colored people. The Author shows the history and
the curse of the N-Word. Unlike any other book, this book
breaks down the word com-
pletely for this generation and
the younger generation of to-
morrow.

THE N WORD

J E R R Y A Y E R S

The N-Word

This book here discusses the real meaning behind the words Nigger, black, African American and colored people. Unlike any other book, this one breaks the word down completely giving the reader full understanding of the word.

The Slave

Similar to "Roots" but this story is a fantasy of what many wish that happened instead. The whites thought that they was profiting off of a slave but later they found out that they captured the wrong slave, the slave that hunted each and every one of them..Horror

Horror Stories

READ AT YOUR OWN RISK

High School Massacre

A young boy who been bullied in school grows up to be a cop and seek revenge on the ones that bullied him.

Love Poems

Poems about love

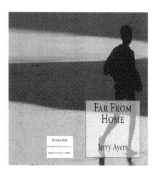
Far From Home

A teenage boy from Nigeria travels to America to further his education but as soon as he got to America, he realize how far he was from home.

School Trip

Teacher's rewards a class of students gets rewarded to go on a special school trip on the last day of school, but they were surprised when they reached their destination. Comedy. Very Funny. A bus ride full of fun.

Caged Bird That Wouldn't Sing

A very touching story that discovers the reality of the justice system...A Caged bird that wouldn't sing is a metaphor and a poetic story that searches for justice within the jail cell. In this story, not all birds belong in the caged.

Hunted by Love

Falling in love is a healthy feeling but it isn't safe, especially not in this story. Not only the cheater says the wrong name when doing it, they may say the wrong name when dreaming...This is a mind twister with a little bit of love, horror, intense, drama and everything else. There's a lot of truth to it, especially when you dreaming or drinking because all the truths comes out.

HoopDreams

A young Street ball Legend takes you on a journey in his HoopDreamz; rising from failure to success and to be recognize as one of the greatest street ball performers of all time. Once this book opens his journey continues.

The Sleep Over

A story about someone who seeks revenge at a family sleepover which was supposed to be a get together party for the family but instead it turned into a terrifying nightmare especially for the younger ones. A story about someone who seeks revenge at a family sleepover that was supposed to be a get together party for the family but it turned into a terrifying nightmare especially for the young ones. A happy family get together party turned into a horror episode once night fell.

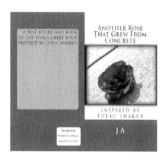

Another Rose

If you read the poem then the story is a must read. A story truly inspired by the greatest Tupac. A best seller and book of the year. This is a book inspired by the late great Tupac Shakur...One of the most interested story you can possibly read. If you read the poem (the rose that grew from concrete) then you need to read the story...This story extends from the original poem by Tupac Shakur (The Rose That Grew From Concrete) to give people a good insight of a rose that really grew from concrete and how it faces obstacles in life because it was looked at as abnormal. Inspired by Tupac Shakur

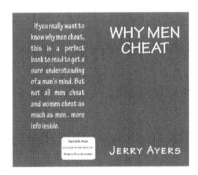

Why Men Cheat

This is a book that every women must read. This can save their marriage and their relationship.

Educational, Spiritual and Healing Poems

Relax and let each poem take you into a different world. You're guaranteed to come back with more wisdom, confidence and appreciation.

Why Do Good Girls Likes Bad Guys

"Why do good girls likes bad guys" is a book that finally concludes the reason it is and speaks the truth about it. It's a story of a good girl who is a model; gets attracted to a bad guy but things turns out bad for someone who thought it was all about love.

16 And Pregnant

If you are 16 and thinking about getting pregnant or have a child that's 16 and pregnant then this book is perfect for you. Very educational for young girls who sees pregnancy as glory at a young age but they learn everything about true experiences of being pregnant. Read the life a young 16 year old who had a baby at 16 and thought her life would change for the better but it changed for the worst. Educational

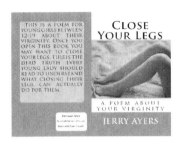

Close Your Legs

This is a poem designed to enlighten younger females about their sexual needs and the importance of their body. Targeted at 12 to 19 year old girls who wants to break the experience only to realize the experience isn't what it really is. If you're a parent and haven't talked to your daughter about sex, well this book talks to them taking every positive word out your mouth. Being a virgin is not a bad thing but can be the best gift for their future and future husband. Once you open this book you may want to close your legs. This is the dead truth every young lady should read to understand what closing their legs can actually do for them.

Bullied

About a young kid being bullied in school. He goes through so much in such a little time. This book is meant to raise bully awareness across the world. This is one of the best bully awareness book in the world. In this terrifying life this kid goes through, he faces bullies, teachers, himself, his parents and his suicidal thoughts.

Legend

This is a poem that defines Tupac influences on the author's lifestyle. A poem truly inspired by Tupac Shakur. The author talks about how he was affected by Tupac's music and poetry to better educate himself for his journey of successfulness. As he explains how every aspect of Pac's qualities helped him shape his personality and become a better person. This is by far the best poem ever dedicated to the life of Tupac Shakur. After you read this book you will have new and more respect for the legend. It's almost like a movie in a book; it's that good.

All monies sold by this book will be donated to the TASF (Tupac Amari Shakur Foundation

Inspiring Philosophies

The most inspirational philosophies written by famous writers and Jerry Ayers. Get inspired, get motivated and get educated by these philosophies. Even better than Shakespeare. This book will change the way you think, will make you happier and will put you in a better mood. When you are feeling down these philosophies will carry you through the day. Share this book with your family and friends and even take it to school and share it with your classmates. It's very educational and a good learning experience.

Love Me More

Jaliah son, Jahsir finds a way to express his love for his mother; but in a way he thought that she would love him more...his mother was left with confusion from the beginning to the end but when she finds out, she's even more shocked. A Mother and Son love story.

Like Sister Like Brother

A mind twisting story about a sister and brother always fighting but something made them realize that they were all that they needed. Once they figured out what they thought they didn't have and realize what they wanted, they gave each other the best thing they can ever give-brotherly and sisterly love.

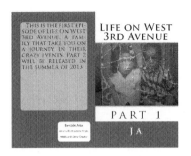

Life on West 3rd Ave

This is the first episode of Life on West 3rd Avenue. A family that take you on a journey in their crazy events.

The Unlucky Summer

This is a story about 2 cousins who been annoyed by their older cousins who came and took over, so they try to make plans to get rid of them, like the kid in home alone (similar story) only learning that they made a bigger mistake and wish they can take everything back...

The Crush

Everybody had that puppy love and everybody had a one year crush but this one is about a young teenager having an unforgiving crush on this special girl in his high school but never could find a way to snap the crush that he had.

Poetic Justice

A poem that describes life in a poetic justice form. The best poem that's probably ever written. Can be compared to Maya Angelou best poems. This poem touches on topics such as poverty, war, justice, racism, prejudice, struggles, ghetto, drugs, sex and everything else that America birthed. A true inspiring poem that can change the complete personality of its reader. Very intellectual and educational. Can be used in public or private schools for further education for students and can be used in colleges.

Funniest Jokes

Treat yourself with the world's funniest jokes

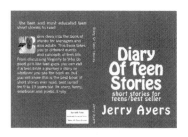

Diary of Teen Stories

Dive deep into the book of stories for teenagers and also adults. This book takes you to different events and concepts of teen life. From discussing Virginity to why do good girls like bad guys. You can call it a teen bible a journey a diary or whatever you see the book as. But you will know this is the best book of short stories ever read. Best suited for 9 to 19 years old. It's scary, funny, emotional and poetic. Enjoy

Basketball Tips & Drills

A complete basketball guide and training book that'll upgrade your b-ball game to a higher level. Learn the secrets of ball handling techniques, shooting techniques, passing, defense, rebounding and much more. Your game is guaranteed to go from a D- to an A+ within a couple of months. It's easy and it's fun.

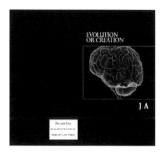

Evolution or Creation

This book is about discussing the topic of "Evolution or Creation". Did we arrive by the big bang or creation? The answers are all in this book. After you read this book your respect for life may change if you have not received the knowledge before. This is also a bestseller in all the book stores. Rated 5 stars by the customers who ordered and left a feedback. In this book you'll learn about Evolution, Creation, Science, the Bible and the Human Brain. And of course you'll find out if there's really a creator or not.

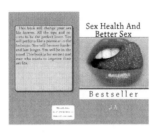

Sex Health & Better Sex

This book will change your sex life in the bedroom forever. This book will help you become like a pornstar in the bedroom. Increases your mood and helps you be very happy. A complete guide to sexual health. Learn to have better sex in the bedroom with over 100 tips and notes. See all the sex positions you can try to make your love life even better. You have Erectile Dysfunction? Don't worry all the secrets and tips of getting a hard on is in here. There's also a list of herbs and natural foods you can take to better your performance in the bedroom. If you're a female who can't get in the mood, well here's a list of things you can do to get genitals up and going. Also learn about all the common STDs that's caused by unsafe sex. And much much more.

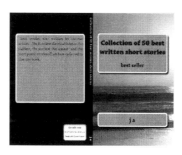

Collection of 50 best Short Stories

The world's best short stories ever written. Written by various famous writers across the world. The funniest, the scariest, the most intense, the most educated and the most poetic stories are all here put together in a collection in this book. You can take this book of stories everywhere you go and show it off. Over one million sold in book stores worldwide. Now it's finally available on Amazon so don't miss out.

Roses

A young lady guided by roses to help her find her lost daughter

Undivided We Fall

Chanel was a pregnant prostitute who sold her body to support her drug addiction, who twin daughters were separated at birth due to a tragic event that took place. Her daughter's grew up not knowing either one of them existed. They both went through their own struggle in life that brought them together as one...... by Gerald Toatley

Printed in Great Britain
by Amazon